The Various
Reasons of Light

Also by Renée Ashley

SALT
Winner of the Brittingham Prize in Poetry, 1991

The Various Reasons of Light

Poems by
Renée Ashley

Avocet Press Inc   New York   1998

Published by
Avocet Press Inc
Suite 400, 635 Madison Avenue
New York, NY 10022
http://www.avocetpress.com

Publisher's Cataloging-in-Publication Data
Library of Congress Catalog Card Number: 98-84310
Ashley, Renée
    78 pp
    Various Reasons of Light : poems / by Renée Ashley - 1st Ed
    ISBN 0-9661072-1-7

Printed in the United States of America
First Edition

Author Photograph: Geneva Studio
Cover Photograph: Win Zibeon

For Ma,
my dear, patient friends,
and, always,
for Jack

Grateful acknowledgment is made to the following publications in which these poems first appeared.

Chelsea: "Where You Go When You Sleep," "Sonnets for the Resurrection," "Velocity of Angels," "The Light, The Dark, The One Stone, and The Bird Looking On," and "One Wing"

Creeping Bent: "July Fourth"

Kenyon Review: "For Brigit in Illinois" and "The Various Reasons of Light"

Negative Capability: "What Makes the Dead Rejoice"

New England Review: "The Generosity of Souls" and "How I Would Steal the Child"

Poetry: "Missing You" and "Pressing the Body On"

Press: "Bending to the Pure"

Southern Poetry Review: "(Five) Untitled Poems: Rain"

Sycamore Review: "Obsolete Angel"

Western Humanities Review: "Entertaining the Angel"

"Sonnets for the Resurrection," "Velocity of Angels," and "The Light, The Dark, The One Stone, and The Bird Looking On" were awarded the 1996 Chelsea Award in Poetry.

"What Makes the Dead Rejoice" was awarded the Eve of St. Agnes Award, *Negative Capability.*

"Sonnets for the Resurrection" and "Entertaining the Angel" won the 1990 Emerging Talent Competition, Judith's Room, NYC.

The Various Reasons of Light was supported by Fellowships from the New Jersey State Council on the Arts, the Corporation of Yaddo, and the Geraldine R. Dodge Foundation. My gratitude to them all.

Contents

I

THE VELOCITY OF ANGELS

I

*Physical concepts are free
creations of the human mind,
and are not, however it may
seem, uniquely determined by
the external world.*
— Albert Einstein
Evolution of Physics
(1938)

My god, how fast she must have fled you
your only, your umbilical angel. How quickly

her going must have passed, how the air
must have parted — her light winking, and she

was gone. How you must have hated the idea
of her.

You can't complain, you know, about

the heart, hers a fiery and weightless thing; your
body was a hindrance to you both, and when you

genuflected at the crucifix of her luminous
breastbone, did she undo you? Was the speed

of her understanding more than your body
could bear?

II

No, your angels don't give you
much time. Their hurriedness unhinges

better men; you read her wrong. And now you miss
the bright widow's peak, the vast white-gold

of her cleavage. The breadth of her sympathetic forehead
was the bed you danced upon. On how many nights, in how

many incarnations did she come to you? You claimed her;
you called her by name. Her fanciful light was a limitless

moon, was the gathered radiance of countless individual stars —
and you are ungrateful. Think hard now: you are the scapegrace

of her dreams. Did you ever really own her?

III

*It takes light eight minutes
to travel from the sun to the
earth, and hence we see the
sun, at any moment, as it
existed eight minutes ago.*
— *F. Capra*
The Tao of Physics
(1975)

You never understood. Look over your head:
the yellow star we dote on could be gone, the speed

of discovery misleading. Factor in the distance;
an incalculable infinity separates us all. She may,

your expeditious angel, hover like a moon-faced doll,
she may be soft and white, may be as fleet

as the crumbs of the universe spiraling outward,
the whole in motion, continual, voracious, the unnamed

space dissolving like sugar on your transient angel's
tongue. You thought she lived to be your small

exuberant god, your *a priori* angel. When she abandoned you,
she left silence as large as her light.

IV

There was a young lady named Bright,
Whose speed was far faster than light;
She set out one day
In a relative way,
And returned home the previous night.
— *Arthur Henry Reginald Buller*
***Punch**, Dec. 19, 1923*

So you dream of speed, of your headlong, prodigal
angel. You seem to have no choice, but your body is a bane,

entropy your body's friend, inertia the solace of your limbs.
Hers is a solipsistic ether; she doesn't even know you. Her
    journey

is breakneck; you stumble, even here on the low, familiar ground,
like the hoodwinked oaf you are — and you would argue

the propinquity of angels? You are full of contradictions.
If you must think of her, think of her heavenward and wearing

white, see her, trembling and brilliant, in the tail of a single star that
    plummets
outside your pitiful, finite boundaries. Your cumbersome body,

that minor eclipse, was her single bright heresy. Render her
your absolute angel; nothing about her is constant

but her speed. You must see it: velocity is her catechism.
Listen: she's your photon, your quantum of deliberate light.

II

FOR BRIGIT IN ILLINOIS

Dear Brigit,
      (Come back.) Here the quiet moon burns
like hayfire over the mountain; the lush rose,
wild as milkweed, burgeons in the dark on the roadside
where, in daylight, you saw yourself in the stark yellow eye
of the grackle. (I never really thought you'd leave.)
Now, your words, dusky as bird wings, rise; you

reckon the distance between our lives — I can hear you
thinking. (What I know is: the good sober will burns
in you like insatiable fire. You never lost it.) The leaves
in May (do you remember?) burst from their delirious twigs
    and rose
sharp as sawteeth in the generous sky. I
thought god had made his glorious point right there, outside

the body, in the visible heaven where the new green sighed
and the air shimmered like the coruscating pond. You
spoke of angels with bodies, the soul focusing its bright eye
on substance, the solace of a promised resurrection, the burning
need for the coming together again (I believed every word).
    We rose
like spirits ourselves, two souls glad of understanding —
    the leaves

about us, above us like dreams. We thought: no one ever
    really leaves.
In this life we were wrong. In this life the issue of where you
    reside
matters (I miss you — the house finch, hungry and rose-
colored, takes his thistle like alms; he is humble and strong.
    You
would like that.) Now, all around me the bright tongue of god
    unfurls and burns
— you must see it in the plains: the gold light of morning,
    the violet dusk. I

trust we still share the vivid heavens; the idea of the
    mountains, I
leave that to recall: the way they rise beneath god's feet, the
    way the leaves
that crown them catch the vast, explosive light, and burn
around and around the countless birds who live invisibly on the
    mountainsides.
(Nothing is the same. The landscape is too big without you.)
I imagine the flat land where you live: linear, predictable,
    innumerable placid rows,

inexhaustible greens, lush golds keen as the level eye of the
    grackle as he rose
and you saw yourself go with him. (We never understood the
    birds, their cold eyes
like small stones, or like glass. The ambivalent fires rage inside
    their hollow bones — you
must understand that now, the way I understand, or think I do, the
    taking leave
of a place you love and the way sorrow, its quiet shadow ebbing,
    one day subsides.)
Nothing is forever. (Come back. Tonight the night burns

in the thousand treetops and the fire leaps even from the pale
    rose, its leaves,
its fine, myriad thorns; it springs from the eyes of the dark sleeping
    birds, from the undersides
of their dark wings. You must close your eyes. Come home
    — we'll watch the red finch burn.)

THE VARIOUS REASONS OF LIGHT

I

Because someone said, "Let's walk," and then the fire
   rose from the heart of the ice, from the jet lake,
and the skaters cut their orbits, apogee, perigee,
   slick stars, a hundred flickerings, quick
in the vertiginous light — the only sound: the blade,
   the lake, their meeting. Behind the coarse sky,
the moon, blind eye like an old nickle, dark
   above the candescent flames, the fire
like amber, molten, imperative, the gold eye
   of possibility and then the snow like a wild dancing.

II

I fall back dazzled . . .
At having, I myself, caused the
sun to rise.
— Edmond Rostand
Chantecler

The paradigm is clear: you are the sun.
  That's it: be the sun. Lift your pale leg
and light sprouts from the rising, from
  the elegant trajectory, lambent and simple,
a crotch of light, day in the simple guise
  of will. Or the sun is attached:
looped tightly over your bony knee,
  a long string snugged about the passionate
star — somber days accounted for, a cinching in,
  the slighter light — a tricky slipknot
you finally mastered. Or it is not will; it is not
  you at all. Vain and short-sighted in the eye
of the awesome sun, you are the light's fool;
  unwary simpleton, you reel.
Tireless in the bright, perfidious beam,
  you are guileless and fluttering.

III

God is an Unutterable
Sigh in the human heart. . .
— Havelock Ellis
Impressions & Comments

Imagine you, cut loose
  from your big heart — slick
fish in your deep chest, red
  as a sailor's moon. Imagine
the heart's shenanigans,
  sealed in the familiar body,
tight beyond the bone, deep
  in the shadow bearing down,
and then the concatenation
  of darkness and the bright day —
the supple effulgence, the secret riot
  of the heart's palaver played out.
Figure in the miracle: the glory
  flashing in the steady hand,
the antiseptic light keen
  as the mute blade, and some god
sighing in the simple, good heart.

(For Louise)

IV

That inescapable animal walks with me,
Has followed me since the black womb . . .
A stupid clown of the spirit's motive,
Perplexes and affronts with his own darkness . . .
— *Delmore Schwartz*
The Heavy Bear Who Goes With Me

Always, over your shoulder, you ogle the darkness.
　When the faint stream of ginger light that lingers
on the dim horizon falters, you rest your faded eyes
　and over your head the Punchinello moon hangs,
a gibbous, homely hunchback loitering, endlessly,
　to one side of your long night — you finally know
the flatulent god who hums your greasy world.
　He belches the round vowel of significance;
the viscous light, the moon's spittle, shifts;
　you watch him do his half-assed arabesque to the tune
of your shallow breathing, to the slow, cautious
　shuffle you dance in his derelict light. To accommodate
his darkness, your pupils swell, rods and cones
　go crazy in your shallow eye; in his slow crawl
after the sun, you run, too wild — flummoxed in his woozy
　glow you grow secretive, your body too weary
to bear the absolute: he will be with you forever.
　You become him, the encephalitic beast that haunts you;
you dance your tired dance, you hobble,
　you hang your pointed hat on the moon.

V

*Before you knew the word dream
and the word fire, you dreamed of fires.*
— Lisel Mueller
Talking to Helen

Ever back to the burning. Before
  you knew your name, before the fire
sealed your eyes, you were aware
  of the flames — your heart whispered
the music they danced to, your pale skin
  wore their shadows like rouge.
You heard it within you: *spiritoso.*
  Obbligato. You named it, never
spoke its name, but it rose inside you —
  heat will rise — and it spoke
from you, the great, urgent furnace
  of your life burst forth, consumed
your silence, overwhelmed even your blindness,
  and you shone *— forte, forte —*
you burned like a white, white sun.

VI

Voracious! You would have god in the deep
  bowl of your eye, in the knob of your bone,
in your sly tongue. You would use him up!
  You, gross glutton, would gobble the exacting
light, guzzle the visible, glorious stream —
  your scrofulous head tipped back, you'd swig
god down.
              Imbecile. Listen, in the wind
you can hear him; his hot breath buoys the clouds,
  buttresses the quiet sky — he's a ravening god,
open-mouthed, insatiable — and you, cupidinous
  idiot, believe you could swallow him whole?
Turn around, take a look: the horizon is his lip.
  Walk quickly — he is fervent. *Famished*
is a mild word for god.

VII

There's light enough for wot
I've got to do.
— Charles Dickens
Oliver Twist

Go, go — gather the stones
  that will mill the wheat, gather
the water in buckets; in fistfuls,
  the grain. Light the fire,
set your pale hands to the leaven.
  Unembellished, the sun and bread
will rise. Press the weight
  of your wanting behind
the sweet dough; knead. Use
  your wiry wrists, your capable
fingers. There is enough light
  to see it through: the sun
is your missal. Awaken and work.

GLASS

              Endlessly, me clattering
            behind you, one ticklish
       step, one brittle shoe, one
          stumble behind — the heart's
          clickety lag, the slick,
     exquisite path . . . See,
            it's tricky in the stunning
                    dark — clear stones
            like potholes, inverted,
  ankle-twisting
       sons-of-guns
          I've got to leap
  over like a goddamn
              stag. It's all so
                  fragile — the delicate road,
              the intricate race.
     Listen, let's grab
        a shard of what you see
          up there — you're
  the wild-assed and prodigal boy.
            I'm merely your tremor,
                your faint, giddy shadow

        watching while you quick-step
over the lightless track.
    But I believe in smithereens.
    I know lucid splinters
when I see them.
        (They tell me
            the sun shines
            white-blue here —
platinum, fulsome &
    blinding.)
    Breathe deeply,
think:
            steady and *stalwart*
                (think: *luminous*) —
        this is perfidious darkness.
You've got to consider
    our common
        glass footprints,
    the lucent rain,
        our common glass,
            our weary hearts.

                            (for Michael Madonick)

(FIVE) UNTITLED POEMS: RAIN

***

The sky is as dense as bread
  — I shake the windows

open, the doors, then
  breathe the thick

magnificient air, and saunter,
  sure-footed, past the defunct

iris, the raging pigeon weed,
  to the road's cusp of lilies

where, in the downpour,
  the awesome tigers

have thrown open
  their wide orange eyes.

***

The spruce is a blue
  shadow; far to my west

the invisible sky explodes,
  somewhere water falling

over water. From beneath
  the scandalous, woven leaves

the indian pipe, the ghost's
  shade, rises and seems

to rush the dollop of sun
  more quickly to the rim.

***

Even my bones covet the shadow
  but the bright sun

swells. We surround ourselves
  with laurel, the shuddering

forest — the delinquent downy,
  the silky red-bellied, both

crazy with the dense warm rain.
  The new pup's nose works

the small breeze. The green air
  is wild — the flicker's

insane siren, the darkening beak
  of the starling in the seed.

***

The old dog catches the scent:
  thunder, thunder and no rain,

the tin sky still, the cowbirds,
  myriad river stones at the myrtle,

at the aster, the ragged azalea.
  By Friday, the steam rises

from the pavement, the grackles
  are dull, wild humidity risen up

through their feathers, clouding
  their yellow eyes. Nothing is dry.

***

The clear voice starts low and rises,
  seems to come from the lilies, then

from the gravel at the edge of the road,
  from the sapling pine, the fiery sumac.

A shred of its weightless song lingers
  between the high rock and the shallows,

rises again, envelops the hilltop,
  lifts even this burdensome,

sulphurous heat, and, in the brittle moment,
  the instant before understanding,

the rain breaks, the air is strung like wire:
  it is August, and Francis is singing.

(for Dennis Grossmann)

III

ENTERTAINING THE ANGEL

She won't eat; even the sweetest, most translucent fruits,
   their glittering liquors, repel her. And she's not
built for dancing. Unworldly, she drifts, evanescent
   above my slick floor, my disheveled bed; she whispers
I can see you. I know what you're thinking.
   Her vague arms are open and strong; she is steady,
ambitious. She is as fine as mist, and always with me.

At first, it was the tremble of her wings that sent me
   speechless, backwards, pitching towards the fall;
it was the stark cricket on her shoulder, hard, real as coal,
   screaking in her celestial ear — an angel's own dark
and crook-legged witness. No one told me she would be there,
   but, still, at the corner of my eye, peripheral and hazy:
an edge of her nebulous hem. I could not know her. And

when she spoke, I thought it was rain, I thought
   the one white birch moved nearer, I thought it was the sound
of the lank ivy growing full before my eyes. I thought
   Be not forgetful of strangers and the angel shifted —
squarely before me she planted her pearly feet in the air,
   her faint feathers were still: *I am your angel, your genius,
your chain. I am the distance you travel.* And she knew me —

all trespass, all omission — the paltry, impossible details.
   She owns me; I am her only diversion. My barnyard of fears
is her playground, my bliss her bliss. She is adamant: No
   to the honey and iris, No to the hornpipe in the riotous street,
to the slight breeze that swings up from the dense, moist
   banks of the river. I say *robin, tango, book.*
Marble. Sunset. Bread. She becomes my hours, my intimations;

she is fraught with me. I breathe her. I think
   embodiment, manifest, God. I behold her borrowed joy,
her immaculate emptiness, behold the cricket, sturdy
   on her shoulder, the dark, seemingly eyeless mote
who keens at the coil of her shimmering ear, who speaks
   through her vast, illumined mouth, whose silence
stirs the violent wind, stirs the angel herself, moves worlds.

PRESSING THE BODY ON

Nothing so simple
  as a single perfect cloud,
    but an infinitude,

nightly, persistently,
  each pausing overhead,
    each, in turn, certain

it defines the word
  cloud.
    And below me, macadam,

or stones, or shallow water,
  the endless ribbon
    passing beneath,

indistinguishable
  from the furnace
    of my breathing,

from the meticulous pumping
  of my heavy bones —
    the earth, black grass

and exquisite rubble,
  the consummate moon
    pale and crisp.

I am the one
  body moving.
    I dream of running,

of endless dawn.

HOW I WOULD STEAL THE CHILD

From the darkness, from his native blindness,
  drag him into my world. Like a dream,

      in a keen, necessary plan — penitent
      and anxious — bathe his limbs, his small head,

feed him the starry milk, own him. Lash
  him to the rim of the grassy shore,

      listen to him breathe; study his closed
      eyes, see the wistful heart in the pulse

at the narrow wrist. Slip him between
  the colors of night, the gradations of dawn;

      he will know nothing. Blank-eyed
      and needy, he will make himself known.

I can save him; he must love me. I have been no
  place, done nothing. I am so ashamed.

JULY FOURTH

Richer than not knowing
 is not seeing: over the lake
the thousand stars

fly into pieces, fire
 fanning the black, black sky —
their clamor is the spur

to the love we make.
 For six days you traveled
far from here, witnessed

the dry, withering place
 you come from. Tonight
you will sleep the sleep

of the tired coming home;
 you'll breathe the humid ash,
pull the dank sheets

from your body
 and turn to face your sleep
alone. I will watch as you

move down, deep
 as the black sky
will be deep when

the detonation
 of this galaxy
is done.

INVENTION: VARIATIONS ON
THE INCREMENTS OF DARKNESS

I

And the sun closed before me
                              (like a box
                                        like a drawer)
                    and all around the night
                              wore darkness
(like an endless robe)
                                        as I wore loneliness
          a blank sky
                              close to the bone
and the arms of the wind
                                        (like a bitter

                                                  child)
              curled (like white smoke)
                    around
                                        nothing
                              and restless (like caged dogs)
it swung
                              (like a fist or a wing)
                    and stilled
                                             before
the whole night slammed shut
                                        (like a door
              like a memory
                    like a small,
                                   fastidious stone)

II

so the geese tucked in sleep
        (like
                perfect stones) —
    and fish leapt
           (like
silver
    music) (like
                the sound of gold
on gold)
        and disappeared:
      still the white
           morning
and alone in it,
       light
   strained
      through god's
           teeth

and the sharp-winged birds
     shivered
        in round trees
      (like worlds)
   — we borrowed
      from the bright pond
          breath
(like deep water
   like cold river)
       (like a blank
    sky)

III

full sun (like

a hammer)

and under the sky

the trees whistled

in the heat — even the faint

silver fish

torpid

(like stone) (like sleeping

or solitude)

and the water (like dusk)

restless

(like some

dream)

but still

to the eye

that wanders

(like geese):

all this

ripe noon

swings

from the water-willows (like stars)

(like moons)

(like glass)

IV

(like a shadow) (like the blood moving)
          swing out, become
                    the slipstream,
                                        the teeth

the tongue —
                              memory
                                        (like a wing)
                    circling back
                                        the circling back
          (like this)
                              (like a round stone rolling)
(like loneliness)
                    the evening
                                        curling in
               the breadth of its dark
                                        arms
its sigh
          (like a sigh)
                                   and
                              your small moon
                    dragging its skirt
                                        (like

smoke)
          (like song):
                              your portion
                                   of earth
                                             hum-
ming
(like wind, like the end of drought)
                              (like a dark night)
          your faultless,
                              improbable stone

WHERE YOU GO WHEN YOU SLEEP

I

It is all conjecture: that dark place you drift to,
its vast ceiling flecked with the light of dreams
    your phototropic senses turn to;
slaphappy with option, you hunger for the wildly improvised
    and open yourself
wide to sleep, to the trek towards the quickened, the
    ephemeral,
the damn-near-tangible understanding of the still sleeping.
You are the dreamer's dreamer, and until you are ransomed
    by wakefulness,
the candor of your passage keeps you solidly on your own.

II

There you go, off along the moonlit road where sleep
streams from you the way filaments of silver trail from the visible
    stars;
your myopic eyes drag it out along the darkness, a single bright
    track
you follow in, your heavy, somnolent feet deep in the teeming light.
You are artless and steady; you want only elbowroom for the
    profligate dream,
would trade decorum for the artifice of the unrealized, for
    sleep riddled with invention.
Overwhelmed and horizontal, again you would refresh your life.

III

This time the stars climb into your bed and carry you across a
    dark
field of sleep woven to the thickness of your dream, and far away
the light and the not light flicker like a familiar, patient eye.
    You travel
empty-handed; you bring nothing you know of with you, carried
    off the way you are,
stolen, so to speak, giving yourself to the theft and grateful for it.
But this time you are sidetracked — your transient stars
    insist — and you are lost between dream
and not dreaming. You reach (you are lucid enough for reaching)
    but the dream
is slippery; unprepared for the stillness and the vastness, you
    slide back again
and find yourself blind in the depth and breadth of fathomless
    sleep, sleep like a cave, like a dark cave.

IV

And there are nights you travel backwards, blindfolded. You
    dream the mother god,
the father — it is different for us all, but the genius of this god is
    facelessness:
this is the worst, the anonymous relic, unnamed and unknowable.
These nights you would flee your dream; these nights fear
like a flame beneath your tongue incites in you the naming of all
    you would choose never
to name — the rocks, the pinnacles you would throw yourself from
if the dream were to take you in waking. You loosen the fabric
    that blinds you,
and yours becomes the desperate eye. And you, the ardent
    dreamer,
struggle for your own unencumbered vision, for your province, for
    a foothold in the culpable dream.

V

In one dream you rise with the archangel to the precious gates
but before you can squeeze past the keeper, a voice repels you
    the way you in your waking lifetime
repel the difficult and the dangerous, and you are jostled,
bit by bit, downward, and, from all around you, all the while you
    fall, the voices
in the gallery applaud your lack of grace in the falling. And this
hoary dream is nearer what you seek, the vehement climbing,
the strain in your groin, thin ribbons of muscle pulled taut in your
    thighs.
But familiar damnation is never enough. Even in your soporous
    need, you know:
better the kamikaze dream, or better the beseeching. Better
the dream in which you tangle with the dark thing in you that squats
    on its spindly haunches
and sees through your eyes. After all, it is only sleep, it is
    only the spidery figment of occasional lapse,
that marrow-like place between what you yearn for and what you
    might find.
Pursuit, then, becomes your obligation, and resolution hunkers
between the slabs of your need, between the finding
and the knowing, between night and the edge of the impious
    dream.

VI

And you lean into sleep as you would a lover, and the ribald
    trickster, fastidious rogue,
in turn takes you in. And love, like the notion of sleep, seems
    cogent and cocksure
and you are certain that your difficulty comes from the sorry fact
that no one told you sleep was concentric, no one explained you
    must go in
and come out, or that sleep is a bull's eye, a wagon wheel, a tin
    can lid
and that it all means nothing if you do not at least consider the
    centermost path.
And you, the ragbag, dissolute lover, still bargain; needy would-be
    libertine, you barter —
bagatelle for the quixotic. Sidestepping the sublime, you pursue
    sleep layered with turmoil;
you, in your ignorance, court the bland space that surrounds the
    ecstatic center
and you pass through the shallow quadratura, the flat concoction
    that passes for dream
at the edge of dream. You go up to and into the heart-stopping
    dark
but there you are stymied. You grope, you paw the black ground;
you are as anxious as a suckling mouth; you are horny with greed,
    and you know the roué,
lousy bastard sleep, like love, is the birthplace of dreams.
You believe you would risk loneliness, every night, you would
    gamble all that you have cast out
or ever taken in, to reach the heedless landscape where everything
    dangerous meets the light.

VII

And, so, how do you find it? What do you make of sleep, of
     your extravagant half-eyed muse,
feathered, dark, incandescent as dusk? You are the starry-eyed
     pilgrim; you mingle
with the shades of her kin. You are rapt with envy for the bursting
     of her bodiless light, for her dream
of the reckless, of the wastrel, and, solitary as the celibate moon,
you shake your fist at the bugbear that haunts you.
The vagaries that befall us all are behind you, and, reaching
     like the footloose beggar you are,
the lucid dream, once more, inevitably, evades you: you
     grasp nothing —
no one ever told you the prerequisite for peace is peace.
You are alone with your appetites; you sleep again.

ONE WING

He tells me he's sad, says
        there's this small angel
floating in his head; he

can call her up and she'll
        come just like that,
dancing. No matter that he's

drunk or unshaved; no, no matter
        that his life is one bad
bus ride and the money

won't come. No matter
        that his calls to other
places won't go through,

he's got this angel —
        and he's got this
sight, he calls *particular*,

so that memory goes
        beyond where memory
might otherwise go: like

this angel who is a morsel,
        he is certain,
of seeing backwards. And

he can summon up
          his father — he can
see that far back — old

father dead before
          the boy was two,
a long time before a most

desperate schedule
          brought him here,
before he was sad.

He remembers that
          hand, a good hand.
Perhaps it's the hand

he conjures to paint,
          this articulate
hand he recalls

so clearly, to turn
          the world
on its edge,

and make the spirits
          tumble out,
make them spin. And

I think the angel
         knows, I think
she'll take him

through the needle
         to heaven.
I think I can

see her: one wing
         is bandaged and she's
pulling him through.

(for John Grazier)

OBSOLETE ANGEL

This one can't fly: he's got
   stubby wings, he's old
as space or time; he's gone
   to fat. And now he even
disregards the omens that he never
   should have learned to read
at all: blistered skies,
   the sticky secrets
in the bowels of toads.
   He's used up his store
of magic, he's half-blind,
   but he's crusty
as good bread and willing:
   in the moonlight,
he struggles up the shadows
   towards god, hears
the wheezing orchestration
   of embodied lives
— he always sings low,
   his one hoarse note,
always tumbles down to where
   we save him again
and again he falls
   like a hailstone
from some heaven
   and we will save him.

IV

WHAT MAKES THE DEAD REJOICE

The warm evenings,
the dusks that drive the living out into the air,

out through their painted doorframes, to where
the lonely dead can get near them, these make

the dead rejoice; and the breezes that cool the skin
of the living are not merely cool breezes but the breath

of a single or a dozen hungry dead remembering
what it was like to be alive. They rub their jaundiced knuckles

together, excite the porous bones the way the living
excite the flesh, and we hear the wooden sound of flickers in the
    oaks,

in the single healthy pine behind the barn, hear them where we
    know
the sap runs thick against the curdled bark and dries in layers,

unimaginably dull to the eye, dries in predictable tracks,
like the molten spewing forth of last words, of apologies,

of sorrow from the mouths of the dying.

The dead especially like
the smoky fires the living build on glassy beaches

or the stark bellies of crowded, electrified mountains; the sacrifice
of infinitesimal motes of burned meats rising in the smoke

pulls even the shiest dead forward. The romantic dead believe
we think of them then, when the sacrifice is made in the unbearable
    heat

and the anxious living gather, the way the mourning will gather,
and they are glad; even the unmourned, implacable dead pretend,

then, even the loneliest of the dead will blend amidst the living,
speak softly over the fleshed-out shoulders of the living and tell
     them

— sincerely — how glad they are to be together again. Even the
     dead
will lie to suit themselves.

              And the dead like honeysuckle.
And the smell of strong tea in glasses that sweat like the rocks

will sweat when the spring thaws the laurel mountain. And babies,
the dead love babies — they are not baleful or sad. The dead

like wild rose when the bloom is freshest and strong; they love
the light rains that slowly penetrate the roots that feed the thorns.

The dead are riddled with belief in themselves. They want
our attention, and we feel the unstable soil beneath our pale feet

shiver, but the dead do not judge. They visit us like the
     unrelenting sparrow
— they are the ubiquitous dead, the invisible dead, the fallible,

the available, the remorseless, rejoicing dead.

MISSING YOU

The nights are long, the days
   long between the nights — no time

for sleep; the sheets are ochre
   with damp, with the one body restless

in the folds, the eyelids
   wide in premonition: another

endless hour. The glorious fruit
   in its wicker bowl's gone

dark and soft. Not even the old dog
   lifts his head at the straw sound

of young skunks close and hungry
   in the rhododendron. We

hear the tree-croakers *peep* their tin
   whistles, the night-crickets *whirr*

in the thick dark — all this, the torn
   eye of the moon, and missing you.

THE LIGHT, THE DARK, THE ONE STONE, AND THE BIRD LOOKING ON

We even die like light — over and over, that long
stumble across the dangerous sky to the blue altar
of the mountains, the invisible streams, the leaping
trout of our hearts moving towards shadow. No one
abstains; this is the absolute motion, the dark
body of the soul emerging — once again: an inverse of
                                        expectation

in the long breathing out of your life. (You expected
your body to sustain you, suspected the sheer beauty of your
                              lucent flesh would prolong
the finite day. But sunup is heartless — we stagger through the
                              light.) Darkness
is judicious ground; in daylight we're blind to the thousand
                              permutations that alter
our design: the silvers, the blues, the shifting and fine
                    vermiculations, one
continuous, unbounded change from intricate shine through the
                                        leap

to extinguish the fire. Think of something solid and cool — a
                              flat stone leap-
frogging the steely water at dusk; think of the stone as god-
                    shaped, irreducible. Expect
nothing from anyone; prepare for a fathomless dark; in one
short sweep, you'll be alone. Ask: what do you fear? What do
                                        you long
for? (Remember the day the light closed around you, a fist
              around a breathless bird?   that altered
your perception of flying — you leaned, that night, into the pillar
                                        of dark

until you, too, were shadows and calm. Yet outside, in the
                                    thicker darkness
invisible mouths cried out like bright knives, like keening. The
                                        voices leapt,
they glistened from the dark trees, from the sheer mountain.)
                                      What alter-
native could you bear? Go back to the stone beneath your heart
                                       — it expects
nothing, not breath, not light; it has no eyes, no wish to see,
                                        belongs
to no one. You come together like that: the light, the dark, the
                                          one

stone, and the bird looking on. You are invented again in the one
remarkable death. Remember what you learned: breath, bird, the
                                    increments of darkness.
You die. We all die. We are the pale moon waning; faint and
                                      headlong
we fall lower and lower in the illimitable sky, and the final
                                      dark leaps,
a reckless demiurge, to whisk us away. Not what we expected
at all. Not the blissful culmination we'd be anxious to alter

our lives for. We figured there'd be fiery gold, an altar
where the sun seemed pale, where we would *be* the flame, and
                                                    everyone
splashed through the river of light — the ultimate body, the
                                        very air. We expected
light flowing from a heaven through us. We forgot the dark
and our center of darkness; we forgot the bird and the stone, saw
                                            only the first leap,
the one that suspended us, hanging like a sigh on the air, in the
                                                            long

drawn-out arc of our lives, in the alternation of light and dark.
And over and again, one to the other, we shimmer and leap —
we go on, expect light to bear us upward as we perceive it, as it
                                            has all along.

SONNETS FOR THE RESURRECTION

I

Listen: the gossip of the dead proclaims
  The prophecy: ten thousand times ten thousand rise
To face the light of God's glass river. Wise
  Dead, who lived likewise, clamor for their names,

The opened book; others take vociferous exception —
  The bedeviled, the rapacious. Too late for sacrifice, too
Soon for joy, they rap their tinny tambourines; in lieu
  Of quiet contemplation, they take to noisy machination.

Imagine them: the unjust and the holy, the righteous
  And the wronged in rapt anticipation, recourse gone —
The crucible, God's judgment, handed down. All men,

All souls, the anxious and the terrified, sped to boundless
  Light or final castigation — the children and the myrmidons,
The unclean, the burdened. They are called, are coming. Listen.

II

First, their laughter. Then from the sugary light
  Some muted apprehension: the numberless children
Rising from the stones, from the hard earth — again
  Their brisk shadows against the gaudy sun, the white

Simple moon. (Most can't imagine being damned, can't
  Begin to comprehend the simplicity of judgement —
The possibility of endless light or everlasting punishment,
  Don't know permanence of any type: dead, alive, or revenant,

Accept continuation and, as in life, seek the castle
  Of the magus, the origins of light, twelve gates,
Twelve pearls. Oblivious to darkness, to history, to hell,

These dead don't see their lives in paradigm or parable —
  They play ring around the constellation, indulge innate
Frivolity. They mock with great fidelity the folderol of angels.)

III

The sluggards rise perplexed, scrape the gravel from their eyes
  And wonder where the hell they've been.
They vaguely recollect the dark, their compost heap of skin
  And hair and bone; they're mildly confounded, despise

What getting up again entails — believe that they've been
  Sleeping hard. That dream of dirt and earth depresses
Them, that loneliness, that damp *cauchemar*. The recesses
  Of their minds complain: they've grown ragged, thin,

They've overslept for something they can't name — wound
  Tightly in their winding sheet of dreams, they've
Missed some significant engagement. Grudgingly they clamber out

To see the other torpid dead; sluggishly they move around —
  Try out their eyes, their heavy legs. They leave behind the grave,
The dark, the safety of their grainy beds, and make a stab at the
    devout.

IV

And the drowned roll out like glistening stones to the shore,
  Suddenly aware of the finite sea, the vast, immediate sky.
Cast into their bodies once more, they realize they're dry,
  They're whole; upright, they drift *en masse*, ignore

Their nakedness; graceful as fish, they stream
  Across the sand in concert with the ocean's psalmody.
These are the quiet, percipient dead, bearing their bodies
  Like pearls. All drawn by water, now they seem

Content to wander unceremoniously, combing beach, then marsh
  Then higher ground for vestiges of their histories —
Seeking out indulgences, finding dispersed memories. Each one

Remembers death with clarity: engulfed within impartial
  Seas, they're drawn this time to more imposing mysteries —
The fount of living waters, the father and the son.

V

This time it's Saturday and the dead refuse
  To rise — they've worked hard being dead,
Need their rest, want to keep their groggy heads
  On their dark, dirt pillows. Nobody who's

Anybody can tell them different: not dark
  Angels, not light ones, not dew worms or dogs
Digging holes. They won't partake in dialogues,
  Not judgments, not standing in lines; part

Of what they really crave is fresh brown bread, thick
  Cream, meringue, and lacking those they choose
To stay spoiling in the ground. They know their sins —

Not one of them is eager to recall a nasty prick
  Of conscience, to live his death again, or to accuse
The grisly book of life of mistaking when a life begins.

VI

Or the dead that morning rise with the sun,
  Button up their bones, brush the dust
From their lidless eyes, and stroll, immodest,
  Past the city square, each one a good samaritan:

The lame lead the blind; the mute retrieve the lost
  From amidst the living. Silent and stolid, they take
Their places in the rows of golden seats, then gaze
  Straight ahead. Some are uneasy; they cross

Their pale legs, lean back and try to recall
  The reason they are waiting. Some dead think
The sun is a wild eye blinking their lives again; awed

By the possibility, or, fearful it's an optical
  Illusion, the worried dead begin to glean by instinct
The difference: the frantic light, the shadow some call God.

VII

So the dead gather like sheep
  And wait, trying out their voices —
The tongueless, the timid rejoice,
  All the dead sing out, finally an end to sleep,

A song again, and sinews and flesh and skin
  And breath. They praise the heavy stones
They laid beneath, all stars, the sturdy sun,
  Their familiar bodies. They remember sin —

Remember blindness. Fingertip to fold of flesh,
  Lip to radiant breast, they bid allegiance
To their kind again — the body's music, that perfection,

And, feverish, its ashy trail parallels the progress
  Of their sun. Each dead makes his dark way. Just once
A man, otherwise erect, bends in grateful genuflection.

BENDING TO THE PURE

You are willowy
        with regret:
                nothing bears
                            you
                        affection,
            the river has
            a bigger heart.
The pale whims
        that prompted you
            sank deep
            with their shadowy
                        stones: you
        would rather
        live apart,
                    laden with relics,
    musty with recall,
                the gray birds meandering
                wild,
    through your hair.
        You hear
                    nothing
    and, burdened
        with unhearing,

                    you
                would rise
          to the bright conformation
                above you.
You
  are misled.
              The passage will
                        be hazy and low:
          the soft curve
                of return
                    will be a
                    sound
              like the alabaster moon,
like the whispery stars
                  turning on their pivots,
        their absolute
                light
            riffling
                  in the corners of your room.

But
          the swerve
                      of your sorrow
                              complete,

                    you'll climb,
          heavy
   with understanding,
                        your serious heart
                            an elipse
               that just
                         misses
   the cusp of water
                    and
                         significant air —
   you will have tried
        too hard.
                        When you are weightless
                             and forgetting,
   then you'll
             bend
                           like the river,
                     take the long
   willow's
             memory
                 as far
                 as the literal shore.

V

THE GENEROSITY OF SOULS

Look at them, there in the moonlight, shedding
the dry sparks of being, sparkling like mica,

like gold, or not shining at all, but heady
with substance, their vague mouths open to the wind

and, indistinguishable from that wind, their edges
the wispy contours of apparition. These are the hallowed

souls, as all souls are hallowed in their partial light,
as all souls starve, wasting in the ravenous wind.

There, wild in the half-faced moon, are the poets
lingering with children and dogs; and those other uneasy

men, excited, insubstantial in the face of more women,
more women than one man's eye could take in in his solitary life.

And despite their restless hunger, the souls are tenacious,
    burdened
by the root strength of the dead, their open hands spread wide as
    fans,

their palms empty, dimensionless. And if, by chance, one thrusts

his blowsy fingers deep into the crisp earth, if he grasps the
    untenable,

or should even one soul fish out of the air the nameless thing it
    seeks,
all souls' hands will gather at that single hand, and dreamy hand

to vapid hand they will eat, reaffirm the glory of substance —
    at that instant
of their coming together their light will quicken, a unanimous

fire, beyond all light, beyond all simpler burning. And if a god,
any god, were to come across them then, he would be blinded and
    stumble;

in his desperation to find his way clear to understanding, the souls
would be lifted from his path, carried from the windy earth

to the calmer place where souls gather in the semi-dark, their holy
spirits risen like dust from the dusty earth to the place

where their giving would be simple as starlight.